ATOM AND VOID

PRINCETON SERIES OF CONTEMPORARY POETS
Rowan Ricardo Phillips, *series editor*

For other titles in the Princeton Series of Contemporary Poets,
see the end of this volume.

By Aaron Fagan

Garage
Echo Train
A Better Place Is Hard to Find
Pretty Soon

ATOM AND VOID

POEMS

Aaron Fagan

PRINCETON UNIVERSITY PRESS
Princeton & Oxford

Copyright © 2025 by Aaron Fagan

Princeton University Press is committed to the protection of copyright and the intellectual property our authors entrust to us. Copyright promotes the progress and integrity of knowledge created by humans. Thank you for supporting free speech and the global exchange of ideas by purchasing an authorized edition of this book. If you wish to reproduce or distribute any part of it in any form, please obtain permission.

Requests for permission to reproduce material from this work should be sent to permissions@press.princeton.edu

The epigraph by Leonora Carrington is an excerpt from "The Happy Corpse Story" (c. 1971). Reprinted by permission of the Estate of Leonora Carrington.

Published by Princeton University Press
41 William Street, Princeton, New Jersey 08540
99 Banbury Road, Oxford OX2 6JX

press.princeton.edu

GPSR Authorized Representative: Easy Access System Europe - Mustamäe tee 50, 10621 Tallinn, Estonia, gpsr.requests@easproject.com

All Rights Reserved

ISBN 9780691278841

ISBN (pbk.) 9780691278865

ISBN (web PDF) 9780691278872

ISBN (e-book) 9780691286051

Library of Congress Control Number: 2025934706

British Library Cataloging-in-Publication Data is available

Editorial: Anne Savarese and Emma Wagh
Production Editorial: Theresa Liu
Text and Jacket / Cover Design: Haley Jin Mee Chung
Production: Lauren Reese
Publicity: Jodi Price and William Pagdatoon
Copyeditor: Jodi Beder

Cover image: © 2025 The Kenneth Noland Foundation / Licensed by VAGA at Artists Rights Society (ARS), NY. Bridgeman Images.

This book has been composed in Adobe Garamond Pro and Scala Sans OT

10 9 8 7 6 5 4 3 2 1

FOR CAMILLA

CONTENTS

Acknowledgments   xi

We Who Are About to Die Salute You   1
Atom and Void   2
Between Things and Words   3
Everyone a Parsifal   4
The Zebra Lounge   5
Cocaine in Sears Tower   6
The Whole of It Calls for Tears   7
Men with Scars on Their Heads   8
Deepfake   9
Aporia   10
Asteriskos   11
A New Way to Pay Old Debts   12
The Passenger   13
The Cloud of Unknowing   14
Rings of Saturn   15
Chronopolis   16
Signs of Things to Come   17
A Last Spark before the Night   18
On a Drive-In Viewing of *The Other Side of the Wind*   19
The Near Future   20
Pretty Soon   21
Intermission   22
An Atlas of Rare and Familiar Color   23
Francisco Goya   24

Interaction of Color   25

Carpets in the Museum   26

Variations of Incomplete Open Cubes   27

A Kind of Life   28

Utter Things Hidden   29

Hedphelym   30

Natural Tuning Green Dusk for Dreams   31

Animal Magnetism   32

I Had to Go Nowhere   33

The Erotic Life of Property   34

Fugue   35

Test Pressing   36

Night Grammar   37

Meditations at Sea Level   38

Hyperion   39

A Clown on Fire   40

Parousia   41

Batrachomyomachia   42

Cascade   43

Pepper's Ghost   44

Anamorphosis   45

Contraption   46

A Beginner's Guide to Invisibility   47

Petals of Fire   48

Stained Glass   49

Exploded View   50

Anamnesis   51

At Capacity   52

The Last Night of the World   53

Maladroit   54

Envoi   55

ACKNOWLEDGMENTS

Acknowledgments are due to the editors of the following publications, in which some of these poems in earlier versions first appeared:

Autre: "Carpets in the Museum"
Bennington Review: "Pepper's Ghost" and "We Who Are About to Die Salute You"
Blazing Stadium: "Cocaine in Sears Tower"
Blush: "I Had to Go Nowhere" and "A Kind of Life"
Cæsura: "At Capacity," "Exploded View," "The Passenger," and "Utter Things Hidden"
Cluny Journal: "Everyone a Parsifal" and "Hyperion"
The Columbia Review: "Cascade"
Grand Journal: "Intermission"
Grotto: "Hyperion" and "Parousia"
Image: "Atom and Void" (titled "Overlooking the Desert")
Liberties: "Animal Magnetism," "An Atlas of Rare and Familiar Color," "Asteriskos," "Interaction of Color," and "The Last Night of the World"
Literary Imagination: "Between Things and Words" and "A New Way to Pay Old Debts"
The London Magazine: "Natural Tuning Green Dusk for Dreams" and "Stained Glass"
The New Republic: "Anamnesis" and "The Erotic Life of Property"
Raritan: "Meditations at Sea Level"
Tourniquet Review: "A Last Spark before the Night"

The poem "Hedphelym" appeared in *You've got so many machines, Richard: An anthology of Aphex Twin poetry* (Broken Sleep Books, 2022). Some of these poems appeared in *Fishing with Electricity* (Old Omen, 2022), *Ni Jury, Ni Récompense* (The Swine, 2022), *Pretty Soon* (Pilot Press, 2023), and *Failure Atlas* (Greying Ghost, 2023).

Knowledge is an old error remembering its youth.
　　—Francis Picabia

Sentimentality is a form of fatigue.
　　—Leonora Carrington

WE WHO ARE ABOUT TO DIE
SALUTE YOU

For starters, my ignorance is what resents what outlasts me.
A friend shares the same story differently every time we meet.
They are all my favorite version. Dense with fairy-tale splendor,
Its premium rises as if a currency. All downturns used to feature
Philoctetes, but that's another story, and the original was lost.
Everyone resumes what they were doing, believing they do things
A little better for each other than they did the day or generation
Before. How then to describe the wars? Not finger puppets aping
Proportion, but as news comes out, there will be a clipping saved
In hopes the situation would improve one day. Heads half-buried
In the sand are unceremoniously exhumed, however, the halfway
Point is a phantom load getting out of hand. But vengeance springs
Eternal where the call to keep appearances kisses history as smoke
Blown in a straw through a cell wall to a lover on the other side.

ATOM AND VOID

The duty of the damned is to be exact.
Candles burn low, thoughts grow clear.
Uncertain how long this night will last,
I open a book, forgetting how to read
The moment the sun begins to shine.
I open the door to go out for a stroll,
But run off like a rider without a horse
All night, hearing flying insects circle,
Chancing thoughts from I don't know
Where, as they crowd upon me, dying
Music I have lost a way to understand.
The tourist trap ends where the river
Enters the sea as outlined in the bargain.
I was never told the soul is not for sale.

BETWEEN THINGS AND WORDS

You can make a man in no time.
A day of joy for a year of trouble.
I grow older but not less wrong.
The errors pile up and compound
My eyes, I have no one to talk to
About interests I have developed,
I am amidst people whose ways
Are not mine, I refuse to be
Troubled by the withering hearts
Of chrysanthemums on the wall.
Seeing too much is seeing too little.
An image passes, then that possesses.
I dismiss this heaven and call it hell.
I belong to the silence of the end.

EVERYONE A PARSIFAL

You have just entered the room;
Our eye contact is a moment old
But my face retains the expression
It held long before you appeared;
There's a flicker of actual time—
Persuasion in a void of reason
Or reality without consequences;
There's an art to doing nothing
As something for something—
A revelation of ordinary love
In majestic images that cure me
Of art for art's sake—a oneness
Of abstract form and feeling—
A spy forever in enemy territory.

THE ZEBRA LOUNGE

Debbie the bartender is drunk and showing off
The lamb-shaped pound cake she made for Easter—
The back legs broken and soaked with Grand Marnier.
Last week, she was studying from her *Gray's Anatomy*
Then turned it in her lap for me to inspect its scale
Diagram of the female reproductive system, tapping
A spot on the page asking: "What's the glans clitoris?"
I turned and wrote: The bar dog, looking starved,
Got tired of loyalty. Tommy the pianist always says,
"Time is fun when you're having flies." He only plays
The opening chords of "Bennie and the Jets" and stops,
Which never fails to piss people off. If a tourist dares
To make a request, he mondegreens the lyrics to insults
Every regular comes to know better than the originals.

COCAINE IN SEARS TOWER

High as fuck and I can't come down, drinking
Whiskey after whiskey, at some kind of party
On the top floor—getting kind of tipsy, kind
Of slurry, I come to mid-screaming at the new
Divorcé who took us here in a hurry with his
Bag of coke, apophenia, and claims he grows
All the tomatoes for McDonald's. He goes on
And on about volume. Says he wants to teach
Me fly fishing, but I know he's intent to fuck
Her. And I know she knows this. I pretend
I don't. I know they know I know. So, I go
To the john, throw up on the borrowed blazer,
Take the elevator down to the street, and hop
The Red Line home in the wrong direction.

THE WHOLE OF IT CALLS FOR TEARS

Just give an honest picture of what went on.
A crowd jumps to its feet. The Texas sky looks
Surgical in its severity, disconnecting the noise
From the brightly colored crowd out shouting
A name at the sky, though I have never heard
The name. That's to say, I see something on
My morning walks with the dogs, as my eyes
Try to adjust from sleep, and then I lose track
Of it, and it doesn't seem to matter. Keep
Quiet and pay the price for paying attention:
You will die looking for a place to die in peace.
I burst into tears years before this happened,
A word circling around me without sound, saying,
You will never know who has died for your sins.

MEN WITH SCARS ON THEIR HEADS

Nothing stays in place
Or rests in peace—
A desire to be taught
What hasn't been done
Before is an erotic riddle.
You wait while they
Change out the lenses.
I find it preferable
To read things I do not
Understand. The brief
Sign that presents itself
To the pitying eye
Promises we will all
See ourselves in the end.

DEEPFAKE

Once you
Realize you
Cannot be
Anything
More than
Who you
Already are,
Why would
You ever
Want to
Let anyone
Know who
You have
Always been?

APORIA

My heart will never
Make me. My heart
Will never make me
Who I am. My heart
Will make me who
I am. My heart will
Make me. My heart
Makes me. My heart
Makes me who I am.
With inexplicable,
Invisible delicacy—
I was driven out here
To forget by a long
And careful mythology.

ASTERISKOS

In what world do you think I would say such a thing?
We waded through possibilities to curb our absurdities.
In youth, I often ran through fearsome rows of corn.
That is not a metaphor. Primary trouble rests its case.
People were after monuments: Less talk, more rock.
A neighbor nearly knifed me open for others to see.
Words are atoms beaten by myriad uses and abuses.
Sweet inevitable, make yourself useful, sing without
Purpose, and time things out in such a way that when
You speak your mind over matter, with catastrophic
Drawl, beautify the plural—its interstices so radiantly
Untrue, a figurehead for all, rinsed of the workaday
Symbols and the impermeable occlusions of power,
Twice-told tales with pages of explanatory notes.

A NEW WAY TO PAY OLD DEBTS

Have you ... have you ever tried in the water, sir?
No, sir, but I swim most exquisitely on land.
Do you intend to practice in the water, sir?
I content myself with the speculative part;
Yet, I aim to build houses from the roof down;
To sow farmland with chaff instead of seed;
To transmute ice, at high temperatures, into
Gunpowder; to soften marble for use in cushions;
To test a subject's loyalty by examining his stool;
To abolish language in favor of talk with objects
To be carried always and everywhere in sacks
Slung across one's back; to extract sunbeams
From cucumbers. I seldom bring anything to use;
It's not my way. Knowledge is my ultimate end.

THE PASSENGER

I try to face the world as it is
And not as I would have it be.
Suffering is a desire for what
Is the case to be other than what
It is—that violent quintessence
Of the romantic impulse toward
Metaphor, the supplanting of one
Thing for another. The way you
Walk into the room tells me some
Of who you are, but there's nothing
Like hearing a person sing, which is
Like listening in on a private phone
Conversation between strangers—
I have put something down to let it go.

THE CLOUD OF UNKNOWING

The solution to most problems
Is to destroy the illusion of clarity.
Before you sing my song,
It must first be burnt to
Ashes so all we have left
Is a theory and a few facts:
Flesh may smile or weep,
But the skull sits stone still
Inside and the twin purpose
Of loss or gain is that we
Arrive, without fail, at
The wrong conclusions.
The story never ends, which
Means the story never changes.

RINGS OF SATURN

I pissed on my face in the mirror.
I am telling you that because I am
Not the man I meant to become.
The solution to most problems
Is to destroy the illusion of clarity.
I know about being shut off from
Primary experience. I try not to
Touch things for fear I will have
To then clean up the fingerprints.
These are mere facts of the seasons.
I never gave up a chance to kiss you.
Those courteous faces in the crowd
Sleep themselves to death waiting
For blood to run cold in the streets.

CHRONOPOLIS

The yellow dress closed in the yellow Pinto door—
Openly sentimental with the naturalness of her way
Of climbing out of experience and into your life—
I do things, too—now I'm breathing, now I'm numb.
The object is suspended in a declension we mistook
For a renaissance. What is it? A gleaming apposite?
I feel the riverbed in my bones, and it makes me sad.
I am used to the deluded permanence I give to things,
One can't do away with what was always there to begin
With, this piece of glass inevitable light passes through
Is a field guide for the centering of inexplicable ideas
On guard, my ears are desensitized to something more
Than the sound of the wind as it exists in the body
Screaming thoughts to itself—inventing perfect horror.

SIGNS OF THINGS TO COME

Echoes of echoes of those
Who loved to rehearse
What was best left behind,
Video copy of a copy until
Only white noise remains.
Invincible passions ignore
Slight changes in repetition.
Suppose there was no song
In the melody you made
Your own, a sigh returning
Through the air gone out
Of the music for good.
I no longer get the book
That changed my life.

A LAST SPARK BEFORE THE NIGHT

If I could plan every horror in advance,
I would've been sure to write you a long
Note on little cards spritzed with perfume
That smells of burnt tires and church incense
To warn you, but I can't, so this will have
To do—my bed of newspapers confirms
A detailed secret everyone knew all along,
The animal kingdom in me comes out
From hiding to hunt and be hunted down,
Taking the sky out of a mourning dove
To sing in the voice of the storm it travels
Through with the aura of an emissary,
Desire gripping the clear promise of a dead
Giveaway I will never know by the signs.

ON A DRIVE-IN VIEWING OF
THE OTHER SIDE OF THE WIND

You can see how these missing scenes tremble against interpretation—
Casting aspersions as you might waking from a pornographic dream,
Who dares enter upon the daylight despairing the nothing there?
Clutch one shimmering image from this rough magic to drive away
The dream one here abjures and never ceases to revel in the loss.
We were told a rumor of collapse upholds stability—as if that's what
We are. Failure involves apotheosis. One—far away, lifting—who
Stayed and died an echo of the age. Sunlight and the dream of sunlight
Keep us from staring. How many words make up the majesty among
Deniers? Unable to fathom what compels me to speak in the clear
Voice of an emperor's auctioneer—the passenger in the body looms
Against another surge made miniature by this monstrous concern:
Knowledge wears us down, and I fear you can only see what's missing
From what is plain to see. Beneath the surface there was nothing.

THE NEAR FUTURE

Soon, a stolen
Letter will be
Hand-delivered
To you at light
Speed across
Light-years to
A place it will
Not arrive on
Time or in one
Piece, but, sad
To say, it
All turns out
The way it was
Meant to be.

PRETTY SOON

The self is lost. One less thing to care about.
As I walked, I held a tiny soft pencil against
The paper folded small inside my pocket.
It has been formulated but not established.
Everyone keeps asking if I can see the cat.
You were meant to eat the fortune cookie
Whole and unread. So little time. I want
It now. Look at the blurry reality. A world
Too real for our sensibility. Find something
Softer. There is a split second from the film
L'Inhumaine that lit the whole gallery pink.
What is real is everything we know is false,
But what we know is currently the best false.
It might be considered less than successful.

INTERMISSION

Instead of going to see an old movie,
We go for a ride. You emit a feeling
That makes anyone in your company
Certain we are all loved by someone.
I have several memories of each place
We have been. There is no reason you
Should remind me of my father's long
Silences, but I miss them now, and not
Because of you—which reminds me
Of how he would get emotional when
He saw a barn had fallen into disrepair.
I miss his sweetness and you are dear
To me in the way he was dear to me.
Absent God, it is nearly inspiring.

AN ATLAS OF RARE AND FAMILIAR COLOR

Movements toward the unexceptional,
Benediction of the voice's mannering
Vagrancy expires to tilt at beatific winds
Tacking ships into a salty harbor of blood.
Let us dispense with muttering receipts
From Pentecostal fire in the chimney
Where the jackdaw builds its nest of straw
For weekend escapes to the empyreal stark.
Ghosts zone out upon the philosopher's stone—
Vacuous processional full of restless spaces.
Charter your tributes to the ritual mystery
Melting fats in a meditation on incarnation.
You wipe your mouth with a piece of gauze,
Steel glittering mirroring messages on the sun.

FRANCISCO GOYA

For Jeanette Hayes

If you put something on the Internet, it's mine. Your mind
Isn't the only thing art damages. Believe none of what you
Hear and half of what you see. The Devoured Son action
Figure takes the cake. I knew that painting was a fucking
Fake. I went to the deep corners of my mind and all I got
Was this enlightenment. Or entitlement? Maybe the real art
Is the friends we made along the way. Two separate men on
Two separate occasions tried robbing banks for my mom.
Both are still in jail. You see, the assassin you sent after me
Is part of my found family now. And there are three messages
In Hello Kitty. First is, you should be loved, and you should
Be nice to others to be loved. And the ribbon represents human
Connections. Also, having no mouth means we need to express
With our actions, not only by words. Those are the meanings.

INTERACTION OF COLOR

Approached each day ready to return
Knowing no knowledge in safety—
Day eventually discovering day,
Nothing is forever new tomorrow.
All along songs that need to grow
On us spring into action unlocking
Stolen loves still too much to bear.
An altar of air colors how hard this
Is to say—your true love remains
Marinated in a marble-box planter
Filled to the rim with Pepto-Bismol.
Composite horrors rendered endless,
Barren minds are full of tendencies.
May we all hang well with our wall art.

CARPETS IN THE MUSEUM

Who cares what your name is or where you're from?
A glance at so-called history proves nothing can be done
Where enlightenment, spiritual education, and similar
Absurdities are concerned. One preaches and is praised
Or spat upon, one is promoted king or sent packing
To the afterlife. And everything will remain the same.
There are surveillances on the other side of our behavior—
Destiny is one thing, amendments among ruins another.
You're already dead if you don't become supernaturally
Cheerful when someone mentions the word *revolution*.
Thousands of years of people who have tried to dress
The part practice prayer and are deformed by form.
Hiding in plain sight, the riddle is the case against us
Explaining the lampless light of an uncaused cause.

VARIATIONS OF INCOMPLETE OPEN CUBES

She slowly entered the room but arrived all at once.
Her smile, in an already forgotten way, tells the truth
About a lie, beautifully. A genealogy of flaws conspires
Behind a common name. Adam's sin is still within us
Miming away—travesties yield, chronicity astonishes,
And love resumes an impenetrable hell resembling
A doctrine fading under a foreign ethic of despair,
And, torn between epitaphs or oracles, bitterness
Hollows out the phosphorous mind's broken mirror
Where the pageantry of exile takes root off-camera—
It's an argument without directions to mislead you.
I dance around the dances of the age—the pattern
Is bizarre, the rest is a mania for what remains
Missing from this worthless amazement of things.

A KIND OF LIFE

I follow the wind in the trees until fast asleep.
Not chaos exactly but maddeningly precise.
How can I not envy its lines and contortions,
This absence that hosts and brings us so near
Here, still in a personal dark without arrival?
Unutterable apologies for cares I cannot name.
Forms tendril away while fixing to narrows.
Impartial elegance devouring the way I feel.
Staged energies compete to pierce the actual.
Are we now finally fully divorced from reality?
It turns out, we turn out the way we turn out.
I hid the details to reveal the feel of details—
As in a realm abstraction might converge upon,
Washing potatoes in ocean water before the fire.

UTTER THINGS HIDDEN

Still nothing new under
The old chaos of the sun,
No idol in the alchemy
Of occurrence to declare,
And beyond the sea at last,
Adapted eyes, with trials
Old as earth, will ends
And aims to consecrate
A face loved for all a face
Is worth, blurred out,
With nothing left to see,
An untitled ray of light
Strains against the waves
Of self-emptying stars.

HEDPHELYM

The telephone rings but no one is there.
A rubber band abandoned by the postbox.
Butterfly wings blocks and weeks apart
Among all kinds of garbage in the streets.
Late last night I told you half my secrets.
A long assortment of empty promises,
Anonymous content in familiar voices.
Pleas to return all of the proceeds fail
To convey data to the inured parties.
The watch at first ran fast now slow.
We sleep and wake all watched over
By unseen machines. A circle invented
The wheel while wisdom slept off
Its catalog of embarrassing wonders.

NATURAL TUNING GREEN DUSK FOR DREAMS

Nothing exciting ever happens here because
I fear I'm alive when I close my closed eyes
As one who may have acquired a new way
Of dying, yet—as my eyes are finally pried
Open for others to see what the matter is—
I am alone dreaming of you unable to wake
Up, and the parts of the lost life we found
Are not lost forever—there's also nothing
Left of the familiar, just a corpse washed
In the community pool dark and clogged
With autumn leaves—a heaping delectation
Of flesh casting a spell on a species of time
Out of season—birth here a single movement,
Pronounced in the way of an elliptical song.

ANIMAL MAGNETISM

Phantom intelligence of the soul knows touch echoes
Trace gestures prone to outcompose their originals—
Springs and veils marvel at a sudden plainness,
Iridescent flies annoy the heads of those about to die.
My stupefaction remains wholly blunt and untamed,
That once-familiar summer will ripen and destroy all
Backward glances aimed at divining an elusive theme,
Leaving room to fall in a series of parallel inclusions.
A scholar of a hallucination taking altar in my brain
Renews a languishing more terrible than perdition.
The storm once more came on fast with annotations
I meant to communicate but haven't written yet—
The dead hang out their songs to cure in the forest.
The gates of heaven and hell are hard to tell apart.

I HAD TO GO NOWHERE

Daydreams rush by as landscapes in a menagerie of light.
I do not know what I'm doing, or how, when I do what I do.
Starved of passion, mercilessness alters desperation feeding
On what it corrodes. All images agree in the dark. Each thing
Bears on its surface a chronicle, form tells form what form
Is, an arbitrary way of being alone, no matter how tenuous,
A construct in a technical dilemma wanting accuracy without
Representation. All points both are and are not an accident:
To know how to make—anything one makes—it's by accident.
Life foresees death, yet hardly lives it out as death foresees,
Transformed by the actual. One knows only a little of what
The point will be. One wants order, but one wants it to come
By rules of chance distractions, a reconstitution of facts tearing
Time away from time with luck and a cocktail of distortions.

THE EROTIC LIFE OF PROPERTY

A truck delivers a forest back to itself
As lumber in the field where it once
Stood as trees—what is not lumber
Listens close, breathes witness into
The absence of what's to become
Of what once was there—closing
The spaces between old shadows
Resolved into new forms, a single
Surface—walls risen from one chaos
Stand alone against another chaos—
Who dares to breathe listens, or goes
Mad against the grain—tilled under,
Folded back against itself—a darkness
In the heart breaks its lost ground.

FUGUE

I can tell you I still see
Him in the hospital bed—
Fluorescent lights distorting
His life like a long film
Full of tiny inaccuracies—
Each frame could be
A standalone photo—
An immense betrayal,
Deranged in scaffolding,
Meant to draw the story
Out—I watch him watch
While the agony beats
The air out of his body
Until he is left alone.

TEST PRESSING

It was all a bullfight in the end—
The smell of death contends
With rain, and more blood
Than we can measure or imagine
Is surrounded by spinning black
Umbrellas—I know the people
Under them by name but not
The one among them who can
Keep memory from calling
On us to crave possession, hum
And nod as another universe
Apes its vivid curse alone—
A voice in distant noise rises
To return in the space between.

NIGHT GRAMMAR

Who knows what has
Happened or that anything
Has—the tides advance
And recede—you can make
The sea sounds say anything,
The still pitiless waves altar
Transcendence, salt preserves
Paradise lost, healing with its
Corrosion, this the only pain
Appeased by the sea's violence,
Hope hollow as the fear
That only the insignificances
One dreams of when
Trying to sing are the song.

MEDITATIONS AT SEA LEVEL

Monuments teeming with weeds
In the heart of picnic-and-fuck
Season drag everything down,
Celebrating the form second
Thoughts take to rephrase—
The bottom of the ocean is another
Shore with new heights to climb
And by heights, I mean depths
Where the mermaid at the heart
Of who I am gives me a push over
The edge in the name of forgiveness
Occulting each event that landed us
Here, where only a perverse delicacy
Survives what we no longer control.

HYPERION

Reverence for a lit match
Plays portal to the volcano—
The funeral pyre pulls us in,
Destruction in renewal charts
A course to force the door
Of a furnace open and enter
Into the mystery of its fire—
Burnt head a globe of pure
Intelligence freely wasted,
The body wears a burning
Gown with dazzling folds—
In the heart of fire, death
Is no longer death consumed
By fire saying farewell to fire.

A CLOWN ON FIRE

Gets a lot of attention, and that doesn't make it a good thing,
Especially if you're the clown, anonymous as the pin:
THINGS OF QUALITY HAVE NO FEAR OF TIME. Late June,
I'm writing an essay in my head about Masaccio's *Expulsion*.
It dives into the old argument that the musculature and use
Of perspective bring dignity to his rendering of the Fall.
It was only recently restored to its original condition,
Before the leaves were added to their bodies in the 1670s.
Groucho Marx and his third wife, Eden, first went
To the Eliots' London home for dinner in June 1964.
A voice from across the room asks, "Are you talking about
The guy with the four-wheeler and the dynamite?" reminding
Me of Vezzoli's *Trailer for a Remake of Gore Vidal's Caligula*,
Animal sacrifice, and people who laugh at the funny parts.

PAROUSIA

I am nature's mistake, some kind of filth only hell knows,
My body is my body of work, and it is a protest aimed
At the librarians of the present and the future—the book
Doesn't bear the name of any publisher and was printed
On stolen paper to show the masks of tragedy and comedy
Overlap—entropy continues to impose fundamental limits
On communication—the elemental ingredient has always
Been surprise—to think: one molecule in the brain decides
A good memory or bad? Your spirit blinded us with twilight
In the mirrored spectrum—you lived, then all the beauty
And the bloodshed won the admiration of the stained-glass
Windows in the Winchester Mansion's grand ballroom
Featuring *Wide unclasp the tables of their thoughts* on one side
And *These same thoughts people this little world* on the other.

BATRACHOMYOMACHIA

Afterthoughts move when you aren't looking—
Anything may happen throughout an occasion:
One's eternal soul demonstrates eternal youth,
Boredom, and nonsense a life cannot survive.
A picture of certain failure, luck will only get
In the way. There is a fossil where one wants
To be or, notwithstanding expectation, divvy
Up our need to blame our hearts for being here.
Easy reasons prefigure graceless astonishments—
Not all signs are disguised under a mask of ashes.
Still the sky burns out with complete illiteracy—
Reduced to a trifle among souvenirs in a window,
A child, who glows in the mind to spell the name,
Sits at a piano searching for a chord never heard.

CASCADE

The coin I carry under
My tongue in death,
Sandwiched between
Two biscuits and honey,
Appears when I come
To along the riverbank
Where my shoes were
Taken off and put back
On backwards to confuse
Whatever might try to
Return along my tracks,
Wash my hair with mud,
And know none of these
Things ever happened.

PEPPER'S GHOST

Dinner will be done soon. She shuts the door behind her.
He gets a huge smile on his face. She blows her nose
With some toilet paper. That doesn't make any sense.
She is screaming at the top of her voice. He places
The egg on the side of her bed. He crosses his legs
And scratches his scalp. She smiles and crosses her legs.
In another room sit a man and a wife who no longer
Remember each other's names. He takes off his shoe
And smells it. She slowly begins brushing her hair.
The birds are chirping, and the wind is blowing.
A Muzak® version of "Eleanor Rigby" plays overhead.
A man is mopping the floor where two kids stand
Licking their large multicolored ice-cream cones.
I figured we could do something unusual for a change.

ANAMORPHOSIS

Are we registering alright on the future?
Nothing must be lost in the back of beyond
Like knowing something about math instead
Of myth. I can always relate to the one who
Wants to leave. Who in their right mind likes
The safety of the shore? You are not the music
Making the new day new. I only know this from
How I bite what I aim to praise in old unknowns,
Now overdone, performed by some grisly new
Version of the mad scientist. Endings can't bear
The way things began because that's not how
It's done anymore—in these supersolitudes
A name appears and lulls to rest the transient
Mind's unexpected comfort craving displeasure.

CONTRAPTION

It's hard to release
The trap you've set
For me—I have an
Ear for the idea
But lost the time—
It is like the last line
Of a song no one
Reads or remembers
Because the lyrics
Are just this unfolding
Of what cannot be
Sung to you in person
In the way in which
I wish I could sing it.

A BEGINNER'S GUIDE TO INVISIBILITY

Acquire the severed head of a man who has committed suicide.
Bury the head with seven black beans on a Wednesday before
Sunrise, and water the ground for seven days with fine brandy.
On the eighth day, the beans will sprout. Persuade a little girl
To pick and shell them. Pop one in your mouth and you will
Turn invisible. If you don't have eight days, gather water from
A fountain at midnight, boil it, and drop in a live black cat.
Let it simmer for a day, fish out what remains, throw the meat
Over your left shoulder, then take the bones and, while looking
In a mirror, place them one by one between the teeth on the left
Side of your mouth. If you're going to fail to disappear, try
Reciting the names of demons in Latin or carrying around a slip
Of paper with twelve numbers arranged in a mystical pattern.
You'll know you've turned invisible when you turn invisible.

PETALS OF FIRE

Craving will end, but it's far too early
In the morning for me to think clearly.
I had nothing to give when you sang me
A song at the top of your lungs, and we
Frightened each other with our laughter.
It's not what we wanted, but it's what
We had, and those are matters I still find
Hard to separate. Everything worthwhile
Ends just before it was scheduled to begin.
A chicken in every pot—a political ploy.
My way to make it new is to make it again.
You don't have to take my word for it—
Pulling the rug from under my own feet,
Going out became as private as staying in.

STAINED GLASS

I hear people are concerned over questions of happiness.
All day, our new neighbors make noise, reminding me
To continue reducing the things I feel compelled to say.
The couple is miserable about not reaching their goals
As if having them sets a kind of alarm to go on upstream
Where no one is equipped to turn it off, and everyone
Thinks this is a reality show just for them, but it's about
The neighbors, remember? Their loneliness, not yours.
The way their light is being spent across the green earth,
Not yours. I walked around for an hour trying to come
Up with a better way to break the news to you but every
Word came out of a mouth inside of a mouth. The hand
Is different, this time, but the note we carry is the same.
No one will ask you what this was about when it's over.

EXPLODED VIEW

I no longer know what it is to love and be loved.
It used to mean weakening and being weakened
By one through subtle extractions from the herd.
The weaker, the better for fealty. Meat is meat
Rendered to a bone willingness for surrender—
Patience lets you wander in your lead leading me
To the place duplicities, enshrined in you, disperse
In ways that may or may not be your own, where
I unmake your plangent desire to penetrate mine—
You act enchanted by the sound of your own voice,
I am love come to destroy history with a callithump.
Who can discern what is distant from what is near?
The dead center moves. The time is always wrong.
Still no idol in the alchemy of occurrence to declare.

ANAMNESIS

Holding up my cyanide cap to the sun, I said,
"A prison becomes a home if you have the key."
It is not the pill but the pink light glinting off
That has me thinking I am in the company
Of God in the form of the pharmacy delivery
Girl standing at my door with a silver ichthys
Necklace also shining a pink beam convincing
Me the Russians have perfected communication
With aliens and I was now standing in the line
Of their transmission like a flashbulb going off.
To say there is no explanation for this is not
An understatement, it is the only explanation.
Put another way: I am the only person to never
Have a mystical experience and remain sane.

AT CAPACITY

Curtains part, we enter
Fleeing the empty promise
Of the human race and exit,
Pursued, without a trace—
Only half of who we are
And twice what we seem,
Timing isn't fair but true,
Strong like animals who
Hide what they treasure
In places they will forget:
Performances decohere
From serenity and order,
This invisible pointing
To the sky is the moon.

THE LAST NIGHT OF THE WORLD

Unfinished dares avoiding rules override Avernus.
Were you wrong about everything to say anything?
Plausible laws insufficient to our lives are blowback
For the myth of liberty. Depeopled palace trumpets
Silent where they were once wild for slaughter calls.
Sons and daughters commandeer our mercy for grief
Discerning: Who would harm a stranger harms me.
Outstare the world's visionary company parched so
Thin on desire and conscience for things as things are
And not as they appear, which appears contradictive
To one who saw dynasties of patience vanish whole:
The golden apple of discord is rotten at the core.
Silence captures how our long shadow-work in sin
Poises eternity for love to comfort us or anyone.

MALADROIT

A bird, dead along
With its song,
Stings your mouth
With burns as you
Approach this pond
To swallow whole
A rippled image
Of the moon—
Echo of old desire
In new passion—
Reflecting light
In cupped palms
You dare to call
The eye of heaven.

ENVOI

One must savor
An inability
To put certain
Appetites into
Words—my
Shadow comes
To look for me
But not for long.
Ignore the case
Of paradise:
A beast hiding
In a cave
Still feels
The sunless rain.

PRINCETON SERIES OF CONTEMPORARY POETS

Almanac: Poems, Austin Smith

An Alternative to Speech, David Lehman

And, Debora Greger

An Apology for Loving the Old Hymns, Jordan Smith

Armenian Papers: Poems 1954–1984, Harry Mathews

At Lake Scugog: Poems, Troy Jollimore

Atom and Void: Poems, Aaron Fagan

Aurora Americana: Poems, Myronn Hardy

Before Our Eyes: New and Selected Poems, 1975–2017, Eleanor Wilner

Before Recollection, Ann Lauterbach

Blessing, Christopher J. Corkery

Boleros, Jay Wright

Carnations: Poems, Anthony Carelli

The Double Witness: Poems, 1970–1976, Ben Belitt

A Drink at the Mirage, Michael J. Rosen

Earthly Delights: Poems, Troy Jollimore

Erosion, Jorie Graham

The Eternal City: Poems, Kathleen Graber

The Expectations of Light, Pattiann Rogers

An Explanation of America, Robert Pinsky

First Nights: Poems, Niall Campbell

Flyover Country: Poems, Austin Smith

For Louis Pasteur, Edgar Bowers

A Glossary of Chickens: Poems, Gary J. Whitehead

Grace Period, Gary Miranda

Hosts and Guests: Poems, Nate Klug

Hybrids of Plants and of Ghosts, Jorie Graham

I entered without words: Poems, Jodie Gladding

In the Absence of Horses, Vicki Hearne

I Was Working: Poems, Ariel Yelen

The Late Wisconsin Spring, John Koethe

Listeners at the Breathing Place, Gary Miranda

Movable Islands: Poems, Debora Greger

The New World, Frederick Turner

The New World: Infinitesimal Epics, Anthony Carelli
Night Talk and Other Poems, Richard Pevear
The 1002nd Night, Debora Greger
Operation Memory, David Lehman
Pass It On, Rachel Hadas
Please make me pretty, I don't want to die: Poems, Tawanda Mulalu
Poems, Alvin Feinman
The Power to Change Geography, Diana O'Hehir
Prickly Moses: Poems, Simon West
Radioactive Starlings: Poems, Myronn Hardy
Rain in Plural: Poems, Fiona Sze-Lorrain
Reservations: Poems, James Richardson
Returning Your Call: Poems, Leonard Nathan
The River Twice: Poems, Kathleen Graber
River Writing: An Eno Journal, James Applewhite
The Ruined Elegance: Poems, Fiona Sze-Lorrain
Sadness and Happiness: Poems, Robert Pinsky
Scaffolding: Poems, Eléna Rivera
Selected Poems, Jay Wright
Shores and Headlands, Emily Grosholz
Signs and Wonders: Poems, Carl Dennis
Stem: Poems, Stella Wong
Stet: Poems, Dora Malech
Syllabus of Errors: Poems, Troy Jollimore
The Tradition, Albert F. Moritz
The Two Yvonnes: Poems, Jessica Greenbaum
The Unstill Ones: Poems, Miller Oberman
A Violence: Poems, Paula Bohince
Visiting Rites, Phyllis Janowitz
Walking Four Ways in the Wind, John Allman
Wall to Wall Speaks, David Mus
A Wandering Island, Karl Kirchwey
The Way Down, John Burt
Whinny Moor Crossing, Judith Moffett
A Woman Under the Surface: Poems and Prose Poems, Alicia Ostriker
Yellow Stars and Ice, Susan Stewart

GPSR Authorized Representative: Easy Access System Europe - Mustamäe tee
50, 10621 Tallinn, Estonia, gpsr.requests@easproject.com

www.ingramcontent.com/pod-product-compliance
Lightning Source LLC
Jackson TN
JSHW021734270825
90013JS00005B/8